Contents

Safety note:
Ask an adult to help you with
the activities in this book.

What are butterflies?

Butterflies are members of the **insect** family. They have brightly coloured wings. Butterflies are insects that can fly. They only fly in the day, not at night.

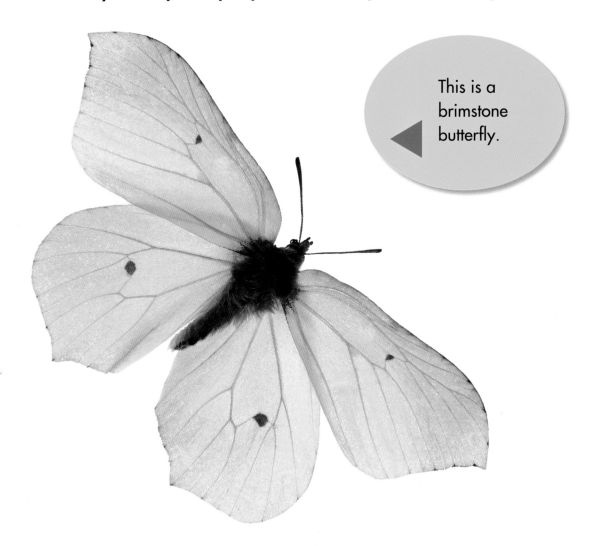

This is a brimstone butterfly.

Grow It Yourself!

Grow Your Own
Butterfly
Farm

John Malam

www.raintreepublishers.co.uk
Visit our website to find out
more information about
Raintree books.

To order:

☎ Phone 0845 6044371

▤ Fax +44 (0) 1865 312263

▣ Email myorders@raintreepublishers.co.uk

Customers from outside the UK please telephone +44 1865 312262

Raintree is an imprint of Capstone Global Library Limited,
a company incorporated in England and Wales having its
registered office at 7 Pilgrim Street, London, EC4V 6LB
– Registered company number: 6695582

Text © Capstone Global Library Limited 2012
First published in hardback in 2012
First published in paperback in 2013
The moral rights of the proprietor have been asserted.

Edited by Daniel Nunn, Rebecca Rissman, and Sian Smith
Designed by Philippa Jenkins
Picture research by Mica Brancic
Production by Victoria Fitzgerald
Originated by Capstone Global Library Ltd
Printed and bound in China by Leo Paper Products Ltd

ISBN 978 1 406 22479 5 (hardback)
15 14 13 12 11
10 9 8 7 6 5 4 3 2 1

ISBN 978 1 406 22486 3 (paperback)
16 15 14 13 12
10 9 8 7 6 5 4 3 2 1

British Library Cataloguing in Publication Data
Malam, John, 1957-
    Grow your own butterfly farm. -- (Grow it yourself!)
    1. Butterfly gardening--Juvenile literature.
    I. Title II. Series
    638.5'789-dc22

Acknowledgements
The author and publisher are grateful to the following for
permission to reproduce copyright material: Alamy pp. 13
(© Linda Kennedy), 16 (© Brian Hoffman), 21 (©
LeighSmithImages), 25 (© Blickwinkel); Photolibrary pp.
15 (Polka Dot Images), 17 (Garden Picture Library/David
Askham), 19 (Garden Picture Library/James Guilliam), 28
(Garden Picture Library/Kevin Dutton); Shutterstock pp. 4
(© Studio Foxy), 5 (© Elizabeth Spencer), 6 (© Ttphoto), 7
(© Tyler Olson), 8 (© Olga Altunina), 9 (© LilKar [Jakez]),
10 (© iladm [Olga Bogatyrenko], 11 (© Antoine Beyeler),
12 (© Inc), 14 (© Margaret M Stewart), 18 (© Trombax),
20 (© Kitigan), 22 (© Vilax), 23 (© Andrew Park), 24
(© Marek Mierzejewski), 26 bottom (© Steve Byland),
26 top (© Lori Skelton), 27 bottom (© Sari ONeal), 27 top
(© James Laurie), 29 (David Dohnal).

Cover photographs of various grasses blossoming on a
meadow reproduced with permission of Shutterstock (©
Sever180), and a monarch butterfly on a mass of white
flowers reproduced with permission of Shutterstock (© Alex
James Bramwell).

Every effort has been made to contact copyright holders
of material reproduced in this book. Any omissions will
be rectified in subsequent printings if notice is given to the
publisher.

To find out about the author, visit his website:
www.johnmalam.co.uk

Disclaimer
All the Internet addresses (URLs) given in this book were valid
at the time of going to press. However, due to the dynamic
nature of the Internet, some addresses may have changed, or
sites may have changed or ceased to exist since publication.
While the author and Publishers regret any inconvenience this
may cause readers, no responsibility for any such changes can
be accepted by either the author or the Publishers.

Some words are shown in bold, **like this**. You can
find out what they mean by looking in the glossary.

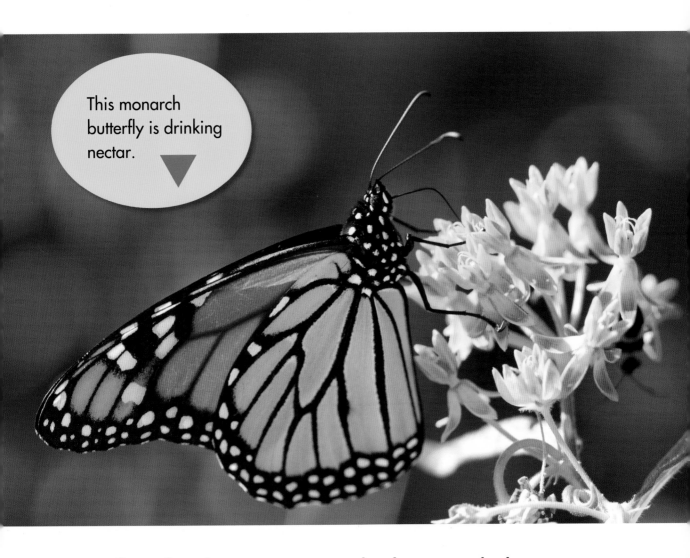

This monarch butterfly is drinking nectar.

Butterflies feed on **nectar**, which is made by flowers. You can grow flowers that will attract butterflies. Many people enjoy watching butterflies in their garden.

What are wild flowers?

Wild flowers are flowers that grow in fields, meadows, and by the roadside. They grow wild, which means they grow where they want to. Butterflies like to feed on wild flowers.

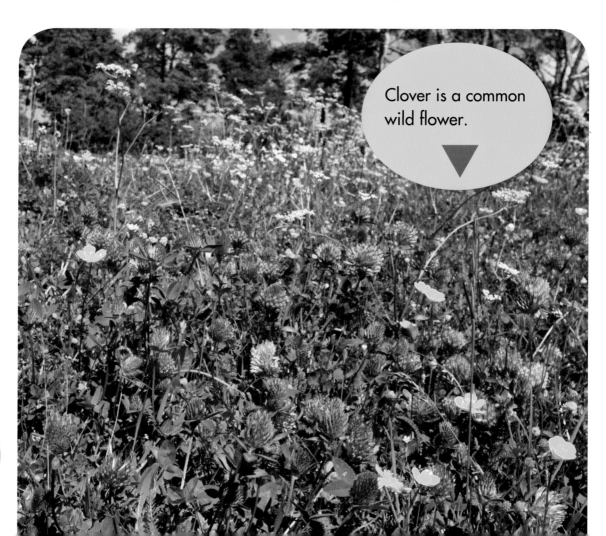

Clover is a common wild flower.

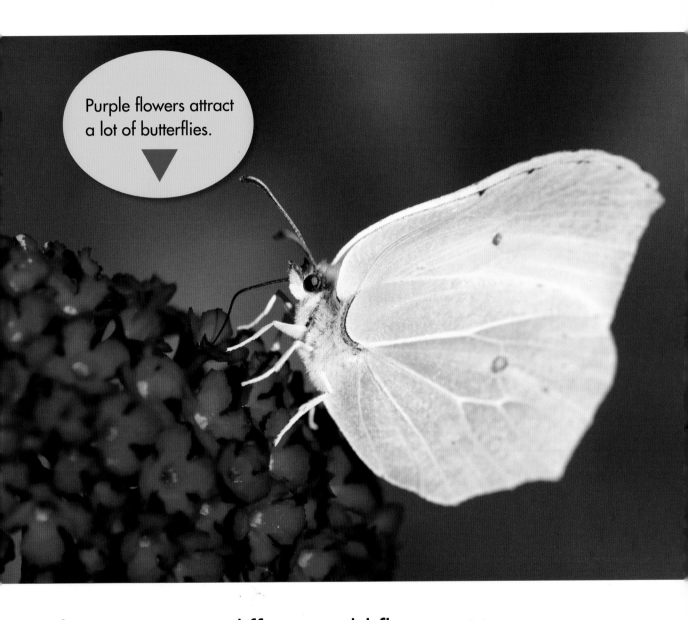

Purple flowers attract a lot of butterflies.

There are many different wild flowers. Here are some you might know: thistle, buttercup, clover, dandelion, foxglove, poppy, and ox eye daisy.

Why do we need butterflies?

Butterflies are good **insects** to have in a garden. When they land on a flower, specks of **pollen** stick to them. They take the pollen to other flowers.

pollen

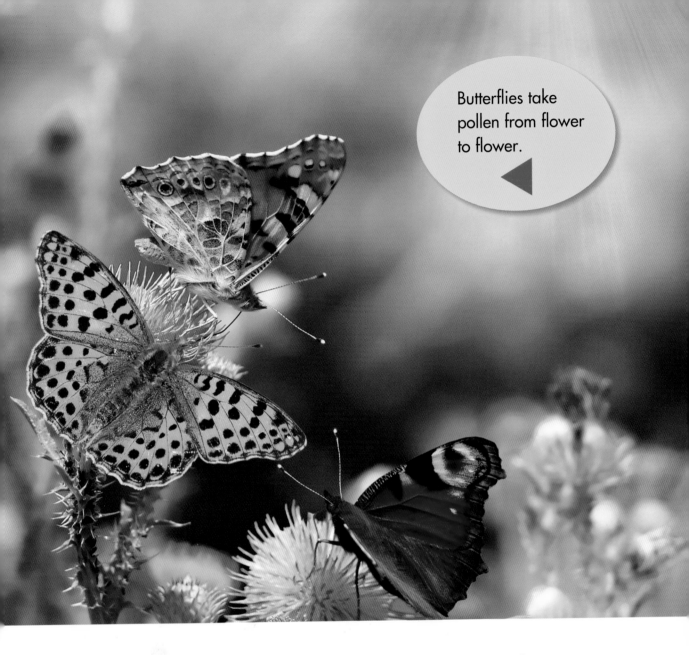

Butterflies take pollen from flower to flower.

Flowers need pollen to make **fruit** and **seeds**.
Insects that move pollen from one flower to another
are called **pollinators**.

What do butterflies eat?

Butterflies cannot chew food. Instead, they are drinkers. They drink water from puddles and ponds, and **nectar** from flowers. Nectar is a sugary liquid made by plants.

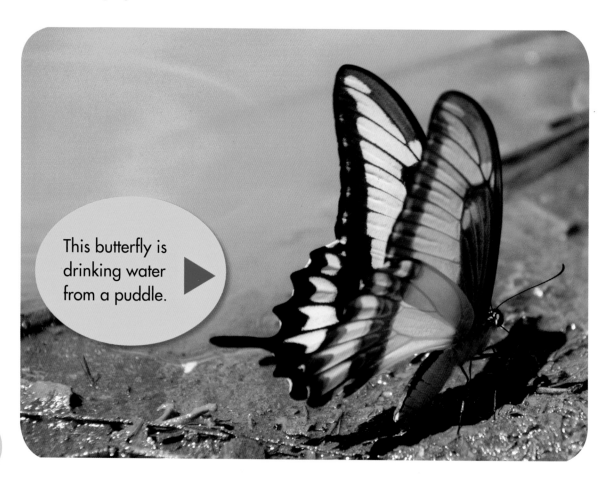

This butterfly is drinking water from a puddle.

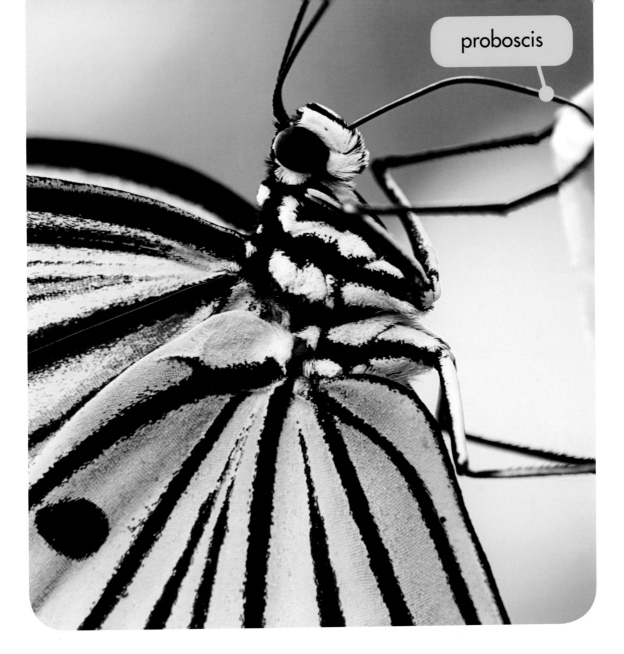

proboscis

Butterflies use a feeding tube to drink through. This is called a **proboscis**. They push it into the nectar or water, then suck up the liquid.

Start your butterfly garden

You can attract butterflies by growing wild flowers. You can grow them in a garden or in a large pot. Wild flowers like to be in the sunshine, so look for a sunny place to grow them.

Find a sunny place for your flowers.

▶

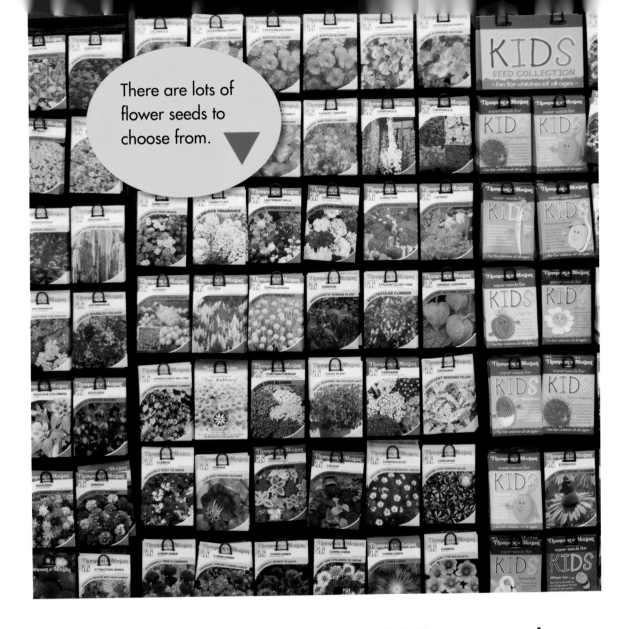

There are lots of flower seeds to choose from.

In the spring, buy a packet of wild flower **seeds**. Look for a packet that says the seeds will grow into plants that butterflies like.

Sow wild flower seeds

In early spring, clear the ground of weeds. Then, make a **seed bed** to **sow** your wild flower seeds in. Loosen the soil with a garden fork. Break up any lumps. Rake it over to make a fine, crumbly soil.

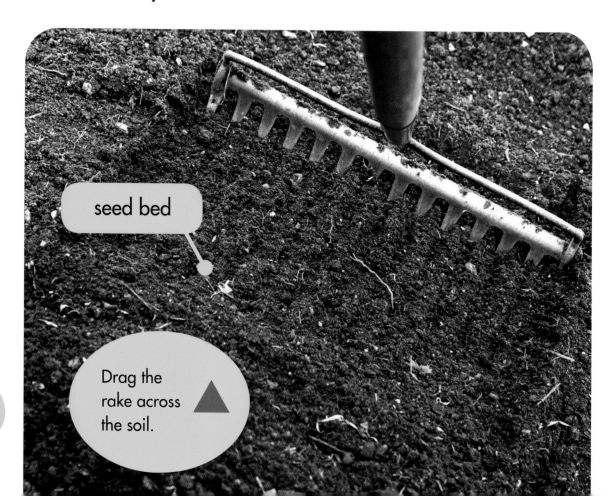

seed bed

Drag the rake across the soil.

Wild flower seeds can be tiny. ▲

Pour a few seeds into your hand. Take little pinches of the seeds and **scatter** them across the seed bed. Use a rake to mix the seeds into the soil. Sprinkle water over the soil with a watering can.

Cats and birds - keep off!

Cats like **seed beds**. They dig up the fine soil, make a mess, and disturb the **seeds**. Birds peck up the seeds and eat them.

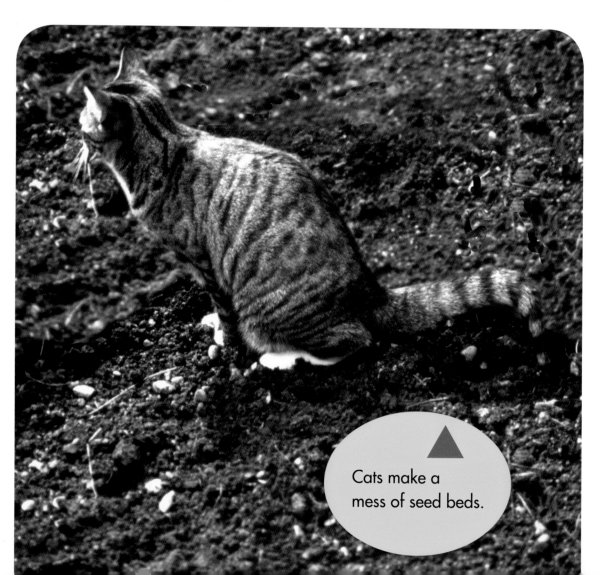

Cats make a mess of seed beds.

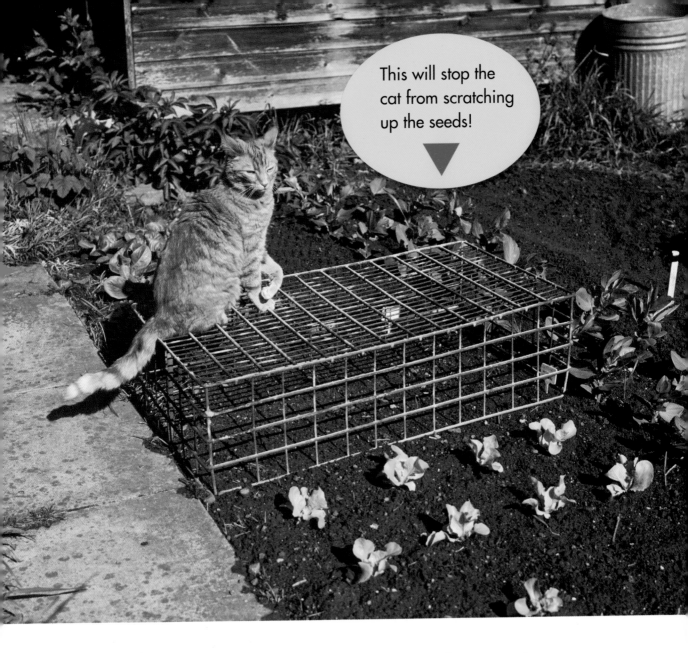

To keep cats and birds away, cover the seeds
with a cage or garden **netting**. You can take this off
when the seeds have grown into small plants.

Watering the seed bed

Keep the **seed bed** watered, especially in dry weather. Try not to let the soil dry out or the **seeds** will not grow. If it has been raining, the rain will have done the watering for you.

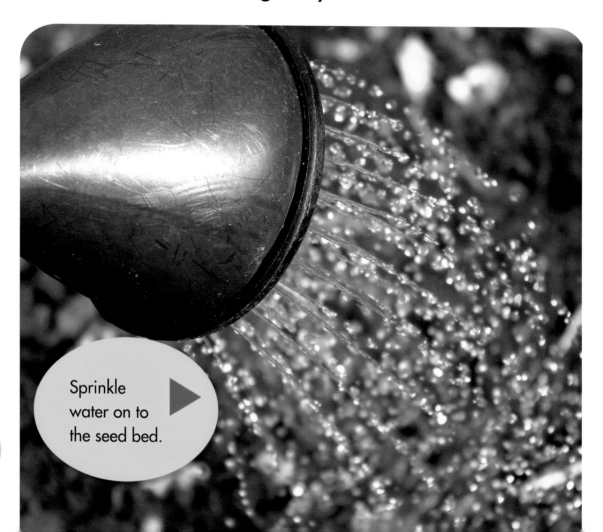

Sprinkle water on to the seed bed. ▶

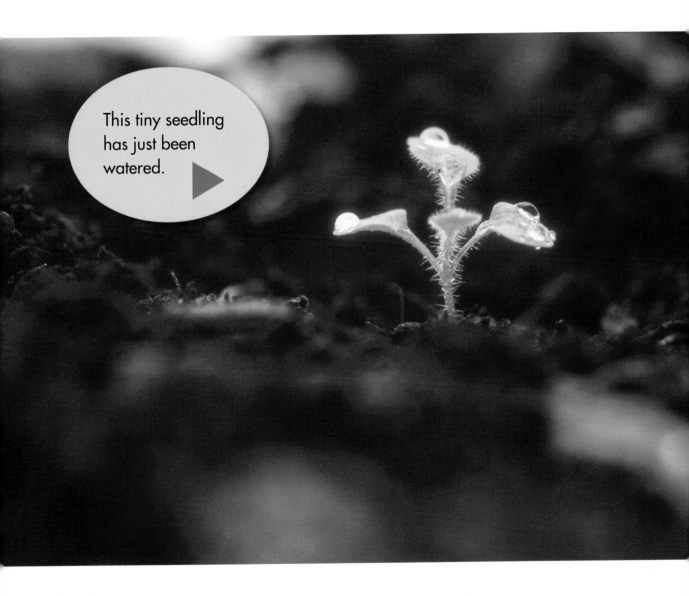

This tiny seedling has just been watered. ▶

After two or three weeks, look out for the tiny leaves of the first **seedlings**. It is often easier to spot them after the soil has been watered.

19

Add some marigolds

Butterflies like flowers that are brightly coloured and stay open all day, such as marigolds. In the spring, garden centres sell trays of baby marigold plants.

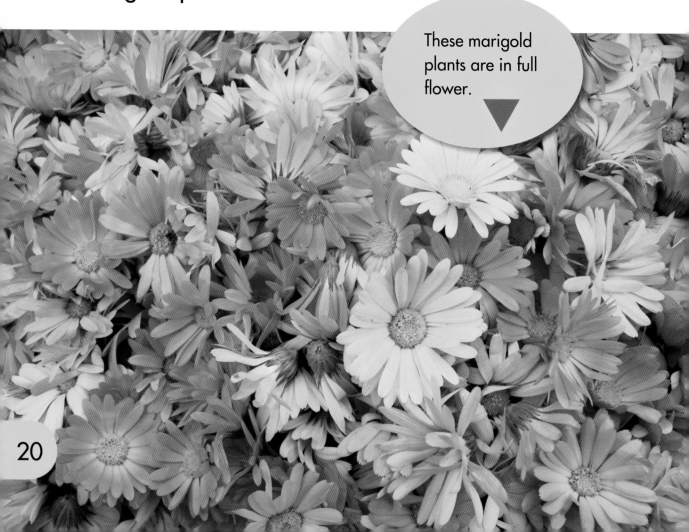

These marigold plants are in full flower.

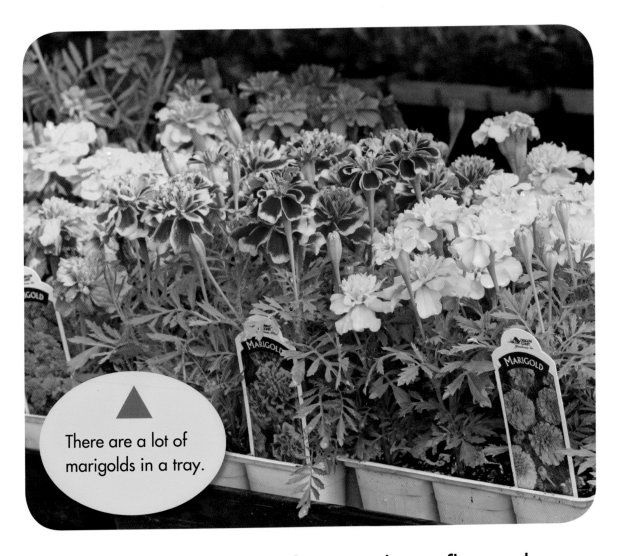

There are a lot of
marigolds in a tray.

Buy a tray of marigolds for your butterfly garden.
Marigolds are shorter plants than most wild flowers,
so put them in front of your wild flowers. This means
you will be able to see them.

Watch your garden grow

Wild flowers grow quickly in the warm months of spring and summer. Some, such as foxgloves and ox eye daisies, will grow tall. Others are shorter, such as forget-me-knots.

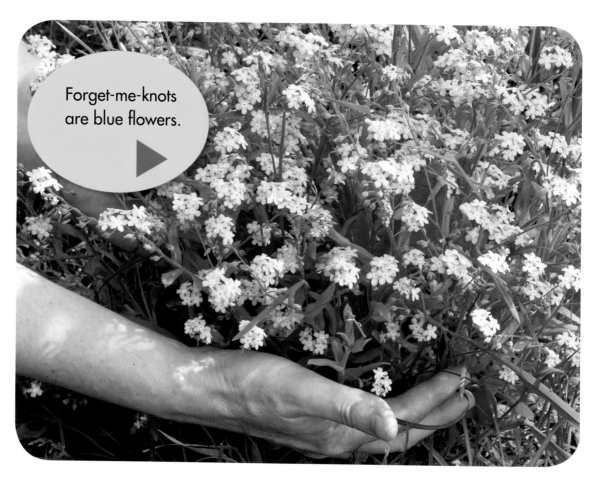

Forget-me-knots are blue flowers. ▶

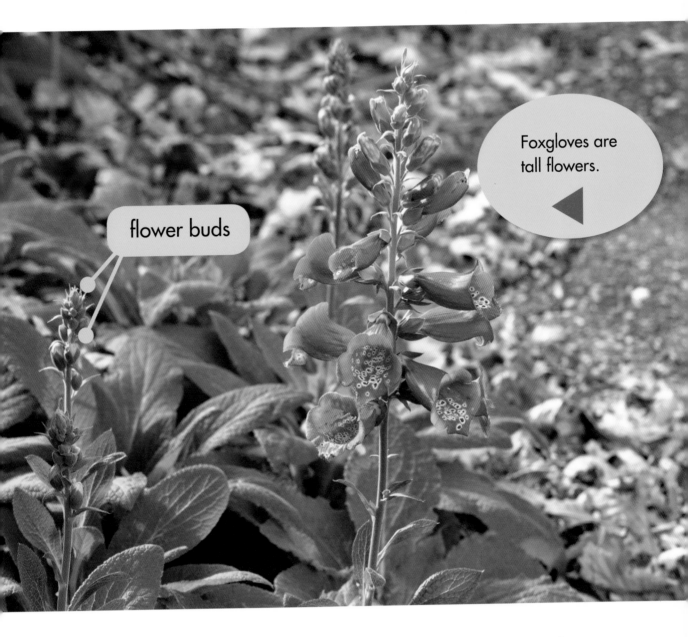

Look for the flower **buds**. Then watch them as they open into flowers over a day or two. Use a wild flower book to identify the flowers you have.

Butterflies have landed!

When the flowers are open, look for butterflies landing on them. Butterflies like flowers that open flat out, so they have somewhere to stand.

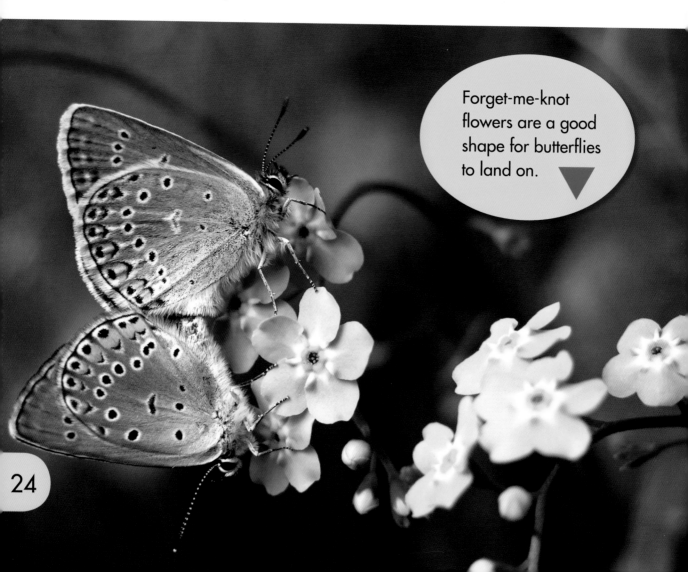

Forget-me-knot flowers are a good shape for butterflies to land on.

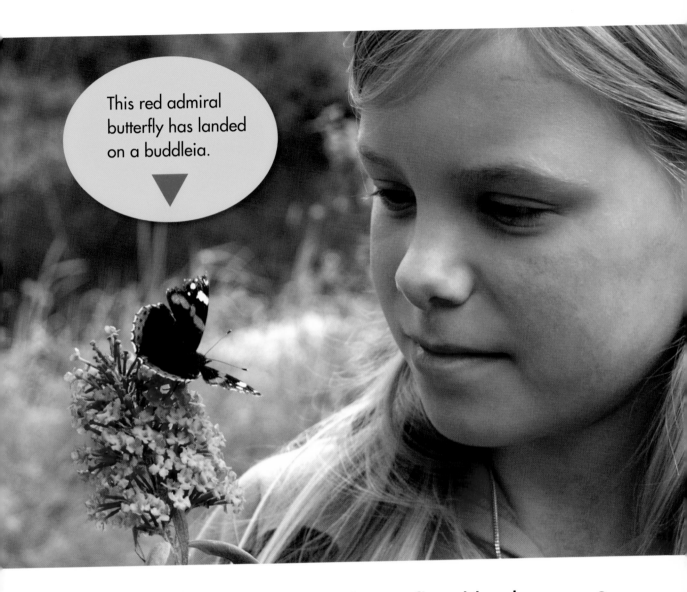

This red admiral butterfly has landed on a buddleia.

What colour flowers do the butterflies like the most? Look closely to see them drinking **nectar** through their feeding tubes.

Be a butterfly spotter

Look closely at the butterflies on the wild flowers.
Look at the colours and patterns on their wings.

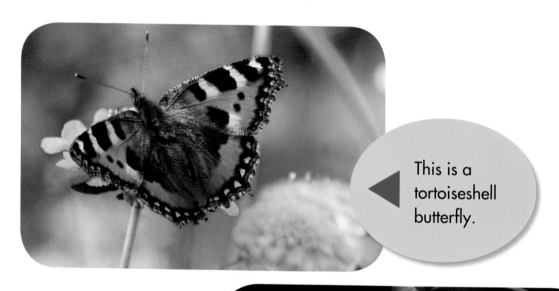

This is a tortoiseshell butterfly.

This is a brimstone butterfly.

This is a purple-edged copper butterfly.

This is a speckled wood butterfly.

Are lots of different kinds of butterflies coming to the flowers, or are they all the same kind? Use a butterfly book to identify the butterflies.

Be a seed saver

Towards the end of summer, the flowers will start to die. Don't pull them up! As they **wither** and dry, the flower heads make **seeds**.

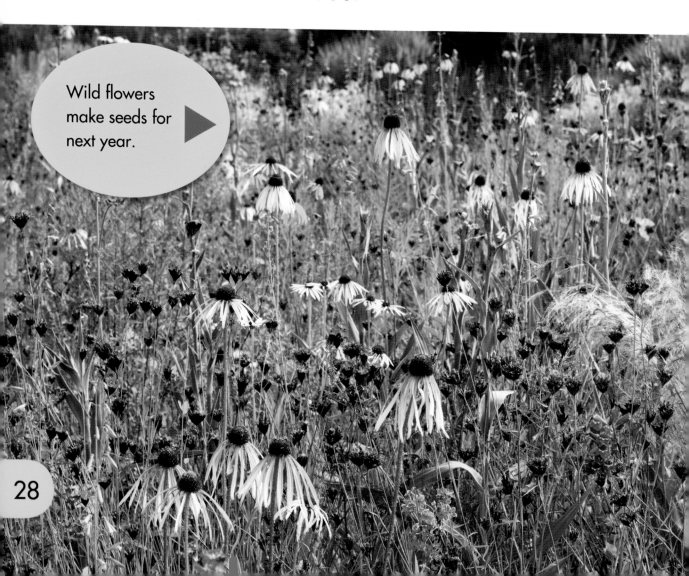

Wild flowers make seeds for next year. ▶

A poppy head holds a lot of seeds.

Shake the plants and the seeds will fall to the ground, ready to grow next year. Or you could pick off the dried flower heads. Keep them in a dry place, and you will have seeds for next year.

Glossary

buds flowers or leaves before they open

fruit the part of a plant which can often be eaten as food. Fruit contains seeds.

insect a small animal with six legs, no backbone, and a body divided into three parts

nectar a sugary liquid made by plants

netting a plastic net with holes in it

pollen tiny powdery grains made by flowers

pollinators animals, such as butterflies and bees, that move pollen from one flower to another

proboscis the feeding tube of a butterfly

scatter to spread seeds across an area by throwing them

seed the part of a plant that grows into a new plant

seed bed an area of fine soil where seeds are sown

seedling a baby plant

sow to plant a seed

wither to shrivel up

Find out more

Books to read

Ben Plants a Butterfly Garden, Kate Petty and Axel Scheffler
(Macmillan Children's Books, 2001)

Butterflies Spotter's Guide, George E. Hyde
(Usborne Publishing, 2006)

Caterpillars and Butterflies, Stephanie Turnbull
(Usborne Publishing, 2007)

Wild Flowers Spotter's Guide, Christopher Humphries
(Usborne Publishing, 2006)

Websites

www.bbc.co.uk/gardening/gardening_with_children/
plantstotry_butterfly.shtml

This website gives you information about creating a butterfly
garden.

www.leadgate-inf.durham.sch.uk/butterflygarden

Find out how a school transformed a patch of land into a
butterfly garden on this website.

Index

Contents

Any words appearing in the text in bold, **like this**, are explained in the glossary.

What is a hurricane?

Hurricanes are the most powerful storms on Earth. They grow from **tropical** storms over the sea. Some stay over the open ocean, far from land, and some weaken and die out before they reach land. Others hurtle towards a shore at high speed.

Hurricane winds often travel at speeds of over 300 kilometres per hour – faster than many of the fastest trains! If hurricanes reach land, their violent, fast winds and heavy rain can cause terrible damage and destruction. Some only last for days, others can go on for weeks. Hurricanes usually cause most damage around coasts, but big hurricanes can sometimes reach far inland.

These waves are being whipped up by a Caribbean hurricane. The word 'hurricane' is said to come from the name of a god of evil, 'Hurican'. People in the Caribbean in the past gave it this name because of its destructive power.

AWESOME FORCES OF NATURE

HOWLING HURRICANES

Revised and updated

Louise and Richard Spilsbury

www.raintreepublishers.co.uk
Visit our website to find out more information about Raintree books.

To order:
☎ Phone 0845 6044371
▤ Fax +44 (0) 1865 312263
▨ Email myorders@capstonepub.co.uk

Customers from outside the UK please telephone +44 1865 312262

Edited by Megan Cotugno, Abby Colich, and Andrew Farrow
Designed by Richard Parker
Original illustrations © Capstone Global Library 2004
Illustrated by Geoff Ward
Picture research by Hannah Taylor
Production by Alison Parsons
Originated by Capstone Global Library Ltd
Printed and bound in China by Leo Paper Products Ltd

ISBN 978 0 431178 73 8 (hardback)
14 13 12 11 10
10 9 8 7 6 5 4 3 2 1

ISBN 978 0 431178 80 6 (paperback)
14 13 12 11 10
10 9 8 7 6 5 4 3 2 1

British Library Cataloguing in Publication Data
Spilsbury, Louise.
  Howling hurricanes. -- 2nd ed. -- (Awesome forces of nature)
  1. Hurricanes--Juvenile literature.
  I. Title II. Series III. Spilsbury, Richard, 1963-
  551.5'52-dc22

Acknowledgements
We would like to thank the following for permission to reproduce photographs: Art Directors & Trip: 4 (Viesti Collection); Capstone Publishers: 26 (Karon Dubke); Corbis: 5 (EPA/Smiley N. Pool), 10 (Reuters), 13 (Dallas Morning News/ Smiley N. Pool), 16 (EPA/Piyal Adhikary); Getty Images: 14 (Mario Villafuerte), 21 (Chris Graythen); NOAA: 8, 25; Panos: 6 (Bruce Paton); Photolibrary: 19 (Index Stock Imagery), 24 (Javier Larrea); Press Association: 20 (AP Photo/John McConnico), 23 (AP Photo/Victor Caivano), 28 (AP Photo); Reuters: 9, 15; Rex Features: 17 (Sipa Press), 27 (Sipa Press); Science Photo Library: 7, 18 (Nasa-Goddard Space Flight Centre); Still Pictures: 22 (Julio Etchart).

Cover photograph of Hurricane Wilma approaching Cancun, Mexico in 2005 reproduced with permission of Reuters (Daniel Aguilar).

We would like to thank Dr. Ramesh Srivastava for his invaluable help in the preparation of this book.

Every effort has been made to contact copyright holders of material reproduced in this book. Any omissions will be rectified in subsequent printings if notice is given to the publishers.

All the Internet addresses (URLs) given in this book were valid at the time of going to press. However, due to the dynamic nature of the Internet, some addresses may have changed, or sites may have changed or ceased to exist since publication. While the author and Publishers regret any inconvenience this may cause readers, no responsibility for any such changes can be accepted by either the author or the Publishers.

This is some of the massive damage to Gilchrist, Texas, USA. It was caused by Hurricane Ike in September 2008.

Hurricanes cause great destruction when they move onto land. They can blow down buildings, pull up trees, and throw cars and boats around like toys. They can whip up the sea to form giant waves that crash onto shores. The strong winds also push massive quantities of water on shore. This is called a **storm surge**. Heavy rains and storm surges can cause floods, when land that is normally dry is covered in water. In the past, hurricanes killed many people. Today **scientists** usually spot dangerous hurricanes early and warn people to move to a safe place.

Top hurricane speeds

No one really knows exactly how fast the fastest hurricanes go because measuring equipment is often destroyed by the hurricane. Some scientists believe that the fastest hurricane winds are around 300 kilometres an hour, while others say they might reach almost 600 kilometres per hour!

How do hurricanes happen?

Hurricanes always begin over warm water. Warm water heats the air just above it and supplies water vapour to it. Water vapour is water in the form of a gas. The warm, moist air is lighter and it rises. As it rises, the water vapour turns back into liquid water to form clouds. When the layer of warm air moves up, cooler air fills the space it has left. This movement causes winds.

Over **tropical** waters that reach very high temperatures, the heat makes the air rise very quickly. As the winds and clouds rise, they move faster and faster. They also start to **rotate** in a spiral. When the winds in this spinning storm reach about 120 kilometres per hour, it is called a hurricane. The whirling pattern of the winds makes the air inside the hurricane move even faster.

Hurricanes may begin like this – as winds that merely whip up waves on the sea. A hurricane usually takes days to develop. The fastest a hurricane might form is two days.

How do hurricanes die?

Hurricanes are created and powered by the heat and water vapour that comes off very warm water. As hurricanes move over land or over cooler parts of the ocean, the supply of water vapour is reduced or cut off and they weaken and start to die out. A hurricane without warm water is like a toy car with a run-down battery – it gradually loses power and then stops altogether.

If fast enough, winds above a warm sea can start spinning within 12 hours. You can see the winds spiralling fast in this picture from above a hurricane, taken from the Space Shuttle.

Naming hurricanes

Scientists give hurricanes boys' and girls' names. They do this so that everyone who talks about a particular hurricane, whether they are scientists or ordinary people, know which one it is. The names go in alphabetical order. For Atlantic hurricanes, scientists don't use Q, U, X, Y or Z as there are few names starting with these letters.

What is a hurricane's eye?

The **eye** of a hurricane is at its centre, inside the swirling mass of wind and cloud. If you could fly high above a hurricane and look down inside it, it would look like water spinning around a plughole. The centre is calm and the strongest winds spin around it in the **eyewall**. When the eye passes over land, people below feel just a gentle breeze and the rain stops. As the hurricane moves on, the winds at the edge of the eye – the eyewall – begin again.

Making a mini-hurricane eye

You can create your own mini-hurricane eye after a bath. When the water spirals around the plug hole, right in the middle there is a dry centre. This is just like the eye of a hurricane, except that in a hurricane you get huge spiralling winds and clouds instead of swirling water.

This is a **satellite** image of Hurricane Katrina. Can you see the eye of the hurricane? Most hurricanes have an eye between 30 and 60 kilometres across.

How do hurricane rains form?

Hurricanes almost always bring very heavy rains. This is because they pick up water vapour as they travel across warm waters. They do this by a process called **evaporation**. The process of evaporation turns liquid water into a gas called water vapour. Evaporation increases rapidly as the liquid water becomes warmer. This is how wet clothes dry outside after washing. The water inside them is warmed by the air and evaporates, leaving the clothes dry.

Water vapour turns back into liquid water when it cools. This is the reverse of evaporation, called **condensation**. In a hurricane, the air cools as it rises. The water vapour then condenses into liquid water and falls out as rain.

Large hurricanes can carry vast amounts of water vapour. This means that they can cause incredibly heavy rainstorms, like this one during Hurricane Keith, which hit Belize in October 2000.

Where do hurricanes happen?

Hurricanes only start over really warm water, so they only form in certain parts of the world. Hurricanes never start over cold oceans, such as the South Atlantic. They form over **tropical** oceans. These areas of water are near the **Equator**, an imaginary line around the centre of the Earth, where it is always very warm.

When is a hurricane not a hurricane?

Hurricanes are called different names in different parts of the world. These storms are called hurricanes when they happen over the North Atlantic and Northeast Pacific oceans. When they occur in the Pacific and Indian Oceans they are called typhoons or cyclones. Even though they have different names, they are the same kind of storm.

This woman stands among the debris caused by Cyclone Nargis. It hit Burma (Myanmar) in May 2008, causing over 145,000 deaths and massive destruction.

Hurricanes on the move

Once a storm has started, it does not stay in one place. Hurricanes can travel thousands of kilometres over the oceans. They move like a spinning top – spiralling around their **eye** at high speeds. At the same time, the whole storm moves slowly forwards or backwards in another direction. Most hurricanes travel generally west or northwards. The average speed for a hurricane to travel is 10 kilometres an hour.

Hurricanes occur in the **northern hemisphere** and cyclones happen mostly in the **southern hemisphere**. Hurricanes and cyclones usually spin in opposite directions. This is because the Earth is turning slowly all the time. As it turns, the winds blowing above Earth's surface are pulled in different directions. The Earth's rotation causes the spin to be clockwise in the northern hemisphere and counter-clockwise in the southern hemisphere.

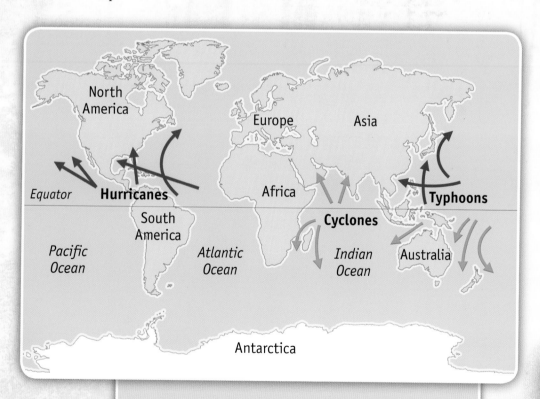

The arrows on this world map show where hurricanes, cyclones, and typhoons usually form and the routes that they usually take.

When do hurricanes happen?

Hurricanes happen every year. There has been a hurricane, cyclone, or typhoon recorded every year for the past 500 years. It is likely that they happened just as regularly before that, too. Every year there is also at least one major hurricane which reaches land somewhere and causes damage or destruction.

Hurricanes always happen at certain times of the year, known as the **hurricane seasons**. In **tropical** oceans and seas, like the Gulf of Mexico and the Caribbean Sea, the hurricane season begins in May or June. In the Atlantic Ocean the season runs from 1 June to 30 November. Hurricane seasons may last up to six months, but the worst storms usually happen over a two-month period – for example, August and September in the northeastern Pacific.

This graph shows the number of hurricanes that have happened at certain times of year over the past century in the Atlantic Ocean, the Caribbean Sea, and the Gulf of Mexico. As you can see, the peak of the hurricane season is from mid-August to late October.

Hurricane Katrina, USA, 2005

Hurricane Katrina hit the gulf coast of the United States on 28 August 2005. It was one of the deadliest and costliest hurricanes in US history. Although many areas were affected, most damage occurred to the city of New Orleans, Louisiana. The city was built on low-lying land and protected by **levees**. The hurricane's **storm surge** pushed water over and through the levees, flooding the city. Officials had asked people to **evacuate**, but many stayed. Afterwards, government response and rescue efforts were disorganized. It was difficult to help the people in need.

> **❝** *'It's like being in a Third World country. We're trying to work without power. Everyone knows we're all in this together. We're just trying to stay alive.'*
>
> Mitch Handrich, a registered nurse manager at Charity Hospital in New Orleans **❞**

Water covers homes just east of downtown New Orleans. Many residents of the area were displaced after the disaster and forced to move elsewhere in the US.

13

What happens in a hurricane?

As a hurricane passes directly over people or places, there are three different stages. First, wind builds up, becoming very fast and bringing heavy rain. Then the wind dies down and the rain stops. This is when the calm centre – the **eye** – of the hurricane passes over. This can last for minutes or even hours, as hurricanes sometimes hover over one place. Then, it moves on and the other side of the hurricane passes over, bringing more fierce winds from the opposite direction and rain.

Hurricanes bring heavy showers of rain. These can cause flooding on land. A hurricane's high winds can whip up high waves that crash onto shores. Hurricanes can also cause **tornadoes**.

Many people have died after going outside while the eye of the storm was passing over, because they thought the hurricane was over. To be safe, people should stay in shelters like this one until the storm is completely over.

Tornadoes

Tornadoes can form in thunderstorms and hurricanes. A tornado is a tall funnel of wind that spins very fast. Tornadoes look like a rope of cloud coming down from a storm cloud. They are smaller and even faster than hurricane winds. Unlike hurricanes, tornadoes can travel far across land. This means they pass over more places where people live, causing lots of damage.

What damage do hurricane winds cause?

Hurricane winds are so fast and strong they can move large objects as easily as blowing a hat off your head. Even the weakest hurricane winds can blow tiles off roofs, rattle windows, and snap branches. The worst hurricanes can blow down trees and move cars and **mobile homes**.

Strong hurricane winds often knock down electricity and telephone cables. This means people cannot use electric lights or cookers and may not be able to call others for help.

Rain damage

Hurricanes can drop huge amounts of rain over a short period of time. A big hurricane can drop so much rain that it causes floods. Floods are when land that is usually dry becomes covered with water. This can happen when rainwater makes rivers so high that the water spills over the sides and onto the land around it.

When floodwater sweeps through a town or city it can damage buildings and bury houses under mud. It drowns people if they cannot get away in time. When floodwater covers fields of **crops** it ruins them and it can also drown farm animals. When this happens it can leave people dangerously short of food.

In 1996, Hurricane Fran dropped huge amounts of rain in Alexandria, Virginia, USA. This heavy rainfall caused serious floods across the region.

What is a storm surge?

When a hurricane gets close to land, the winds can push a high wall of water in front of them. This is called a **storm surge**. When this kind of wave hits land it can cause terrible damage to the coastline.

Storm surges can change the whole shape of the land. They may destroy beaches by dragging the sand and rocks out to sea. Sometimes they dump sand and create new beaches. Finally, storm surges can also cover land and cause floods.

HURRICANE FACTS

These are things that people should do in a hurricane:

1 Stay indoors and keep away from windows.

2 If electricity is cut off, use torches to see in the dark. Do not use candles, which can cause fires if they are blown over.

3 Listen to radio or TV reports and take the advice given by experts and emergency services.

The combination of winds, rain, and storm surges causes terrible damage. In 1996, Hurricane Fran ruined thousands of homes and flattened millions of trees up to 240 kilometres inland from the sea in North Carolina, USA.

Hurricane Andrew, USA, 1992

The first hurricane in the US **hurricane season** of 1992 arrived in southern Florida on 24 August. It was named Hurricane Andrew. Hurricane Andrew's winds were spiralling at about 280 kilometres per hour and it was travelling across land at about 30 kilometres per hour. As it moved over the warm waters of the Gulf of Mexico it gained strength. It only began to weaken as it travelled over land across the state of Louisiana. Hurricane Andrew caused over 60 deaths and huge amounts of damage.

> " *'I've lived through ten hurricanes in my lifetime, and this is going to be the worst. I'm scared. I won't lie to you. I am scared.'*
>
> Louisiana cafe worker, Janice Semien "

This picture, taken over a period of four days, shows the movements of Hurricane Andrew between 23 and 26 August 1992.

What damage did Hurricane Andrew cause?

Andrew turned out to be one of America's most expensive hurricanes. Out at sea it churned up high waves, which toppled **oil platforms** and badly damaged **oil wells**. When it passed over coastlines, **storm surges** smashed millions of dollars' worth of boats and ships moored in the water.

The buildings and many other structures that Hurricane Andrew damaged or destroyed cost over 20 billion US dollars to mend or rebuild.

Scientists who were following the movements of the hurricane were able to warn people it was coming. About 2 million people were **evacuated** – they left their homes to stay somewhere safer. The hurricane damaged or destroyed houses, **mobile homes**, businesses, bridges, and roads. It also badly damaged the Louisiana fishing industry. Over 184 million fish were killed in one area alone!

Who helps after a hurricane?

After a hurricane has passed over, the danger does not end. Most people who die because of a hurricane drown in floods. Emergency service workers, such as fire rescue workers and the **armed forces**, get people to a safe place.

Other workers, from local hospitals and **aid organizations** like the Red Cross, set up first-aid stations to treat wounds. They also set up shelters where people who have been **evacuated** from their homes can stay. They give **evacuees** blankets, water, food, and any medical supplies they need. Emergency workers travel around the area to fix fallen electric power lines that could **electrocute** people, and cut down damaged trees that could fall on them.

Sometimes rescue workers have to lift people out of dangerous fast-flowing flood water caused by hurricanes. This child was rescued from floods caused by Hurricane Hortense in Puerto Rico in September 1996.

Rich and poor

It takes time to put things back to normal after a hurricane. Bridges and buildings have to be rebuilt or mended. Water companies mend broken **sewage** and water pipes. Government workers clean roads of obstructions such as mud, broken branches, and wrecked signs. Generally, people in rich, **developed countries** recover fairly quickly.

In a **developing country**, flooding from a hurricane can cause more long-term suffering. Poorer families usually do not have **insurance** or savings to pay for repairs. If their **crops** are ruined, they may starve. Aid organizations, such as Oxfam, and the governments of other countries send help. They may supply farm equipment, seeds, and farm animals. They may also send building equipment, so that people can rebuild their homes themselves.

Local residents in Pasadena, Texas, USA receive government **aid** after Hurricane Ike in September 2008.

CASE STUDY

Hurricane Mitch, Central America, 1998

In October 1998 a terrible hurricane raged across Central America. Winds up to 250 kilometres per hour swept through, bringing torrential rains up to 46 centimetres in one day. Hurricane Mitch left over 9000 people dead, many missing, and millions more people without homes. Roads and bridges were wrecked by the storm. Floods ruined farmland, many **crops**, and people's food stores. Heavy rains caused **landslides** too. A landslide is when mud and rock slide down a hill causing great damage.

> **"** *'Some neighbourhoods were flooded by water up to 1.5 metres high. People screamed asking for help and some of us, helped by tyre inner-tubes, threw ourselves in [the water] to rescue those trapped in their homes.'*
>
> Roberto Ramos, a Honduran nurse **"**

GUATEMALA

HONDURAS

EL SALVADOR

NICARAGUA

KEY
— Mitch

Many people in Central America work on banana plantations (farms) like this. Hurricane Mitch destroyed most of the country's banana plants. This meant that many people lost their jobs and their chance of earning money to look after their families.

Long-term support

At first, **aid organizations** such as Oxfam and the Red Cross helped by giving people food, water, medical treatment, and somewhere to stay. They also helped people find family members who got lost in all the chaos.

Later their main aim was to get farms working again. That way people could feed themselves, without having to rely on help from other people. Aid organizations worked with local groups to plan what to do. Gradually, they helped people grow new corn, rice, bean, and banana plants to eat and sell. The poorest people in the area were the worst affected. Their houses were flimsy and had been completely wrecked by the hurricane. Aid organizations helped people build new, stronger homes, as well as new wells, bridges, and roads.

Many banana plantations had to be replanted with baby banana plants after the entire crop was destroyed by Hurricane Mitch in October 1998.

23

Can hurricanes be predicted?

Predicting hurricanes is difficult because each one grows and moves differently. Some countries spend a lot of money on **scientists** and equipment to try to work out when and where hurricanes might happen. If they can work out where a hurricane is heading, they can tell people in that area to **evacuate**.

Satellite pictures

Weather **satellites** are special computers that are sent out into space. From space they photograph the clouds high above the Earth. This helps scientists on Earth to predict the weather. Hurricane experts study these pictures to see if there are any clouds that look like they could become hurricanes. They also use powerful supercomputers. These examine weather and hurricane information from around the world to help them with their predictions.

A scientist in Spain uses a computer linked to a weather satellite to view images of hurricanes. Predicting these huge storms is difficult, but new technology is continuing to make accuracy possible.

Hurricane hunters

When dangerous-looking storm clouds are spotted, hurricane hunters go to look at them. These people fly planes all around and into storms and hurricanes. They have special equipment to take measurements and pictures of the weather inside the storm.

For example, they drop miniature weather stations into a hurricane's **eyewall** on a parachute. This measures things like temperature, **humidity**, and wind speed. It sends the information to experts' computers. The experts look at this information along with satellite pictures and facts about the way that hurricanes in the past grew. This helps them to work out how strong a hurricane is and which way it is likely to go.

This is a National Oceanic and Atmospheric Administration (NOAA)-operated Gulfstream IV-SP. The primary purpose of this jet is to assist in hurricane surveillance.

Can people prepare for hurricanes?

When **scientists** predict a hurricane, they send out warnings on TV and radio. If it is a very dangerous hurricane this gives people time to **evacuate**. If it is a weaker hurricane this gives people time to prepare for the storm. Most people who live in areas where there is a danger of hurricanes make some preparations in advance.

Long-term preparations

People can do several things to make their houses safer. For example, they can fix strong shutters to their windows. When these are closed, they stop hurricane winds shattering the glass. People also cut down dead branches or trees. In hurricanes these can cause a lot of damage when they snap off and blow about.

These are some essentials in an emergency disaster relief kit. Before **hurricane season**, governments tell people to stock up on supplies.

All animals must be kept safe as well, before and during a hurricane. People should take pets with them to their local shelter or evacuation area.

Governments can prepare for hurricanes further ahead, when planning new structures such as buildings and bridges. They can make stronger buildings that can cope with strong winds and rain. They can put important buildings, such as hospitals, further inland where they are safer from hurricanes. They can also build bigger storm drains that allow large amounts of water to soak away. This means that future floods will not be so deep.

HURRICANE FACTS

If a hurricane is on its way, but not one strong enough that people need to evacuate, there are still a number of steps that they should take:

❶ People should check their portable radio has batteries.

❷ They should bring in or tie down loose objects outside, such as garden furniture.

❸ They should close windows and shutters.

❹ They should move food and other supplies into the basement or cellar (or the lowest room of the house) where people will be during the storm.

Can hurricanes be prevented?

People have tried to prevent hurricanes in the past. In 1947, **scientists** tried to weaken a hurricane over water near America. They flew planes into the storm and dropped dry ice into the clouds to try to cool and calm it before it reached the shore. It did not work! Scientists today are working on new ideas, but we may never be able to stop hurricanes.

Scientists have learned a great deal about how hurricanes work. This is important, especially when more and more people are building homes near coastlines. Although it is impossible to predict all hurricanes, tracking and warning systems can help to save lives. They give people time to escape and lessen the damage these awesome forces of nature can cause.

In 1935 a hurricane hit Florida Keys, USA, killing around 408 people. In 1960 Hurricane Donna (right) hit the same area. Even though many more people were living there, early warnings meant that only three people died this time.

Howling hurricanes of the past

Galveston Hurricane, 1900
Storm-surge waves 4.5 metres high swamped the whole of Galveston city and parts of the Texas coast in the USA. Around 8000 people died.

Great Miami Hurricane, 1926
This storm caused over 100 million US dollars of damage in Florida, USA. If the same storm were to happen today it would cause over 80 billion US dollars of damage because there are so many more people living in Florida now!

Great Atlantic Hurricane, 1944
This major hurricane hit the eastern US coast. Over 20 centimetres of rain and 200-kilometre-per-hour winds caused 46 deaths on land and even more at sea.

Hurricane Camille, 1969
Huge floods struck after as much as 70 centimetres of rain fell in 5 hours when this hurricane hit the Mississippi Gulf Coast, USA, killing over 250 people.

Cyclone Tracy, 1974
This hurricane hit Darwin, Australia, on Christmas Day morning, 1974. A total of 65 people were killed and 112 more were seriously injured. Around 80 per cent of Darwin's homes were destroyed.

Hurricane David, 1979
This hurricane caused over 1 billion US dollars' worth of damage to Dominica and the Dominican Republic in the Caribbean. Over 2000 people were killed.

Typhoon Ike, 1984
Over a million people became homeless after Typhoon Ike hit the Philippines.

Hurricane Ike, 2008
Hurricane Ike was the largest known hurricane, measuring 1,000 km wide. It devastated Central America and the United States Gulf Coast region.

Cyclone Nargis, 2008
This deadly cyclone hit Burma (Myanmar) in May 2008. Over 145,000 people were killed and massive destruction was caused.

Glossary

aid help given as money, medicine, food or other essential items

aid organizations groups that raise money and provide help for people in need

armed forces army, air force and navy. These forces have equipment to fight with, but also help rescue people at other times.

condensation when water vapour turns into liquid water

crops plants grown to eat and to sell, such as rice and bananas

developed countries richer countries of the world that have well-developed services for their people, such as good hospitals and emergency services

developing countries poorer countries of the world that are gradually developing better conditions for their people

electrocute injure or kill with electricity

Equator imaginary line around the centre of the Earth

evacuate when people move from a dangerous place to somewhere safe

evacuee someone who moves from a dangerous place to somewhere safe

evaporate when water turns from liquid into a vapour (a gas in the air)

eye calm centre of a hurricane

eyewall edge of the eye of a hurricane

humidity when the weather is very warm and moist at the same time

hurricane season some areas have hurricanes every year at about the same time. This is called the hurricane season.

insurance when people pay money regularly to a company that pays the full cost of rebuilding their home or business if it is damaged or destroyed

landslides when heavy rains and wind make large amounts of mud and rock slide down a hill or mountain

levees raised walls or banks at the edge of a river

mobile home home that can be moved using lorries. Most mobile homes look a bit like big caravans without wheels.

northern hemisphere everywhere on the Earth north of the Equator

oil platform/well an oil platform is a building at sea around an oil well. An oil well is a deep narrow hole drilled to release oil found underground.

rotate spin or turn around

satellite object in space that sends out TV signals or takes photographs

scientists people who study aspects of the world around us

sewage waste from lavatories

southern hemisphere everywhere on the Earth south of the Equator

storm surge when the sea becomes high along a coast due to storm winds

tornadoes strong whirlwinds that move quickly over land

tropical in the tropics – regions around the Equator that have hot and humid weather

Find out more

Books

Graphic Natural Disasters: Hurricanes, Gary Jeffrey (Franklin Watts , 2010)

Natural Disasters: Hurricanes and Tornadoes, Richard and Louise Spilsbury (Wayland, 2010)

Our Angry Planet: Hurricanes, Anne Rooney (Franklin Watts, 2009)

Violent Skies: Hurricanes, Chris Oxlade (Raintree Publishers, 2005)

What on Earth: Hurricanes, Catherine Chambers (Book House, 2006)

Wild Weather: Hurricane, Catherine Chambers (Heinemann Library, 2008)

Websites

www.howstuffworks.com/hurricane.htm – to find out more about how hurricanes work go to the hurricane pages.

www.nhc.noaa.gov – read up about America's national hurricane centre if you want to know more about tracking hurricanes.

www.fema.gov/kids/hurr.htm– for facts about hurricane dangers, what to do, quizzes, and more.

http://kids.earth.nasa.gov/archive/hurricane/index.html– go right inside the eye of a hurricane with the hurricane hunters!

Index